'18

Proud of You!

Ramon

The problem is not aiming too high and failing;

it is aiming too low and succeeding.

Michelangelo

The

Illusion

of

Good Enough

Inside the minds of unconventional leaders,
entrepreneurs, independent thinkers, business
mavericks, artists, and outstanding students
and how they defy conformity, reject
society's conditioning of average and
good enough, and pursue excellence
in life through the pursuit of artistry.

Randall Phillips Kunkel

Sherwood Publications, Colorado Springs (catalyst.rk@icloud.com)

Ordering Information
Individual Sales: Amazon, lulu.com
Educational & Quantity Sales: contact Sherwood Publications

ISBN: 978-1-329-08151-2

Printed in the United States of America

Contents

Dedicated to

Ron Wisner (1942-2010)

Brother-In-Spirit

Your Invitation to Possibility

To be nobody but yourself in a world which is doing its best,
night and day, to make you everybody else,
means to fight the hardest battle
any human being can fight;
and never stop fighting.
e e cummings

The Illusion of Good Enough

Let's start with a few key questions that will help you think about how you think.

When did you first knowingly do less than what you knew was possible in some activity because you believed it was good enough? When did you realize that getting by was good enough and was acceptable by many, if not most, of the people around you? When did you unknowingly give up on pursuing what was possible and merely settle for what you had done at that point in time?

To be clear, there are times when we need to complete a task as well as we can due to time limitations, scarce resources, or possible safety issues. These select situations or necessary circumstances are understandable and good enough is appropriate.

What I am referring to, however, is the acceptance of good enough as a way of thinking and approaching life as a normal way of thinking. I'm focusing on the mentality, the mindset, of doing only what is adequate, average, even mediocre, across the range of life situations.

I suggest that good enough is the default standard of what most people find acceptable. Most actions defined by good enough meet minimum standards. In this context, good enough is a paradox, a contradiction, by deceiving you into settling for a reduced expectation of what is possible for yourself and for others. You become conditioned to think of good enough as achievement and give up on striving for higher goals.

Sometime early in life you begin to expect less for yourself and, in turn, lose your awareness of what you believed you were capable of achieving. Now you often adapt to what others think you can or should do. You unconsciously allow outside influences to override your internal sense of who you are and what, in your finest moments, you can accomplish. You conform. You live in the *illusion* of accepting less and believing that is only what is possible for you.

Insights into Human Behavior

My research and work in human behavior have focused on three questions:

1. Why do some individuals with good education, clear opportunities, and many resources consistently make poor decisions and produce mediocre results in work and life?

2. Why do other individuals, facing difficult obstacles and overwhelming odds in life, produce excellence in their work and life and lead themselves and others to high performance and sustained accomplishment?

3. What are the factors that can offset the conditioning to conform to average or below and instead inspire us to excel, achieve, and live more effective, contributing, and fulfilling lives?

Research and Conclusions

My conclusions in this book are based on interviews, surveys, and observations, combined with feedback from consultations, field projects, workshops, retreats, and training sessions over the past 36 years.

I have been fortunate to work with diverse and talented people whose minds, gifts, and personas create excellence and outstanding achievements. Their ability to maintain commitment and high performance often under extremely challenging circumstances is impressive and inspiring. They pursue their best, a sense of artistry, in all their endeavors, professional and personal. Note that they continually *pursue* their best, acknowledging that their current best is what they have previously achieved, and with training, learning, and sustained effort, a new best awaits them. They constantly challenge their own experiences and expand their thinking, skills, and accomplishments. They see their lives as on-going journeys and do not accept any level of achievement as a reason to stop learning and growing.

On the other hand, I often encounter individuals whose attitudes and performances are sub par and disappointing and who seem only to do the least required of them. They accept who they are as static and show little interest in personal development unless it guarantees promotion or a reward of some kind.

Both types of these individuals, in their own way, contribute to this writing about human behavior, performance, and achievement.

The Pursuit of Possibility

My passion centers on the art and science of pursuing possibility. I am fascinated with what the human mind can influence us to do.

My study, training, and research have taken me deep into dimensions of human performance and achievement **in business, healthcare, education, the arts, sports, and non-profits.** I'm convinced that we have immeasurable potential to achieve and are unconsciously conditioned to underperform.

I've extensively researched and pursued *how* to decrease factors that limit performance and increase strategies for self-achievement and a balanced, fulfilling life.

I share here what I believe can inspire you, regardless of your life situation, to challenge your current beliefs, expect and achieve more for yourself, and make a greater contribution to others and to society.

It's not that you need to be extraordinary, rather that you pursue what's possible, do ordinary things with creativity and excellence, persist through challenging circumstances, make your life experience richer and more meaningful, and have positive impact on those around you.

This book is about inspiring yourself and others, lifting the human spirit, and improving the human condition.

I

From Best to Just Good Enough

The Young Achieve The Impossible

Born into innocence, newborns revel in a constant state of discovery. Dreams, imagination, and great expectations fill a child's mind. Each day is a wonder, an adventure, something exciting. Each moment is an experience in initiative, independent thinking, and high energy.

Children are rebels *with* a cause from day one. They have unbounded enthusiasm and are fascinated by the newness of everything they encounter. Their minds focus constantly on possibility.

Conforming and Compromising

Somewhere in adolescent years, however, this exciting discovery of life begins to change. Insistent life messages such as "can't," "don't," "be quiet," and "don't ask" appear more and more. Other messages from family members and peer groups are often critical and blaming, making unwarranted, harsh judgments of themselves, their friends, and other people.

These types of messages take their toll and, unaware of what is happening, children began to conform by thinking, believing, and acting like others rather than continuing to march to their own drumbeat. Their thinking then narrows and other people assume a stronger influence over their thoughts, perceptions, and actions.

So they compromise and adapt.

A child's world is fresh and new and beautiful,
full of wonder and excitement.
It is our misfortune that for most of us that clear-eyed vision,
that true instinct for what is beautiful and awe-inspiring,
is dimmed and even lost before we reach adulthood.
If I had influence with the good fairy
who is supposed to preside over the christening of all children,
I should ask that her gift to each child in the world
be a sense of wonder so indestructible
that it would last throughout life,
as an unfailing antidote against the boredom
and disenchantment of later years,
the sterile preoccupation with things that are artificial,
the alienation from the sources of our strength. [1]

[1] Rachel Carson, *The Sense of Wonder*, (New York: Harper & Row Publishers, 1965), 42-43.

There is not a question of whether children conform. It's a matter of *how much* they are conditioned to think and act according to external influences rather than their true selves. While there are a few stalwarts who develop a strong self-awareness and have the advice, mentoring, and strength to offset some of the conditioning, most children *unknowingly* fall into lock step and follow someone else's drumbeat.

The late Gordon MacKenzie was a creative designer for Hallmark Cards. Mr. MacKenzie visited elementary schools to introduce children to the joy of design. He often told the story that when he would introduce himself as an artist, he would look at the walls of the classroom and see numerous paintings and drawings by the children and ask, "How many artists are there here?"

The kids mostly answered the same way. In kindergarten and first grade classes, all of the children quickly raised their hands. In second grade classes, about three fourths of the children raised their hands, although somewhat slower. In third grade classes, only a few children held up their hands tentatively. And, in the sixth grade classes, not a single hand was raised. In fact, the children merely looked around to see if anybody in the class would admit to what they had now learned was abnormal behavior. [2]

---

[2] Gordon MacKenzie, *Orbiting The Giant Hairball*, (New York: Viking Penguin, 1998), 19-20.

Settling for Good Enough

The restrictive messages and limited thinking of many people children encounter accumulate throughout elementary school years and the excitement of dreaming, risking, and learning decreases. The young minds, formerly so curious and active, lose interest and tune out.

After several years of this regimentation, street-wise young teens emerge, more rigid, righteous, protective, and defensive. External influences have taken over previously independent thinking and produced a thought process often swayed by outside opinion, evaluation, and feedback. Inquiry into possibility is replaced with learning to get by and a theme of *good enough* becomes a mantra. Good enough is a belief system defined by average and mediocrity and is the basis for making excuses and blaming outside factors for poor performance and lack of achievement. Good enough thinking is a convenient way to avoid personal responsibility for one's behavior.

Most of the time, a youngster is unaware of limiting thoughts and beliefs, and the lowering of expectations of what is possible. Over time, children learn to hold back, live smaller, and play it safe.

Good enough becomes a default way of thinking, accepting the experiences of average and normal and the path *more traveled*. So children follow the crowd, believing in the illusion of good enough and allowing average to be acceptable. The young mind becomes numb to the troubling insight of W. Somerset Maugham's words that "only a mediocre person is always at his best."

I had applied for the nuclear submarine program, and Admiral Rickover was interviewing me for the job. It was the first time I met Admiral Rickover, though I was quite aware of his legend, and we sat in a large room by ourselves for more than two hours, and he let me choose any subjects I wished to discuss.

Very carefully, I chose those (subjects) about which I knew most at the time - current events, seamanship, music, literature, naval tactics, electronics, gunnery - and he began to ask me a series of questions of increasing difficulty. In each instance, he soon proved that I knew relatively little about the subject I had chosen.
He always looked right into my eyes, and he never smiled. I was saturated with cold sweat.

Finally, he asked me a question and I thought I could redeem myself. He said, "How did you stand in your class at the Naval Academy?" Since I had completed my sophomore year at Georgia Tech before entering Annapolis as a plebe, I had done very well, and I swelled my chest with pride and answered, "Sir, I stood fifty-ninth in a class of 820."

I sat back to wait for the congratulations which never came.

Instead, the question came: "Did you do your best?"

I started to say, Yes, sir," but I remembered who this was, and recalled several of the many times at the Academy when I could have learned more about our allies, our enemies, weapons, strategy, and so forth. I was just human. I finally gulped and said, "No, sir, I didn't always do my best.'"

He looked at me for a long time, and then turned his chair around to end the interview. He asked one final question, which I have never been able to forget or to answer.

He said, "Why not?"

I sat there for a while, shaken, and then slowly left the room.[3]

---

[3] Jimmy Carter, *Why Not The Best?*, New York: Bantam Books, 1976.

II

What Happens If You Believe You're Good Enough?

Inside every old person
is a young person wondering what happened.
Terry Prachett

Cause: The Forces of Limitation

A number of oppressive influences impact our thoughts, beliefs, and actions from our earliest years and subsequently throughout adulthood. Those that have the strongest influence include:

1. Dysfunctional People and Relationships
2. Suppressive Cultures and Environments
3. Pervasive Negative Media
4. Our Own Unhealthy Lifestyles

1. Dysfunctional People and Relationships. Dysfunctional behaviors of conflict, negativity, judgment, blaming, and criticism are pervasive throughout society. We observe and often personally experience this in politics, business, education, sports, religion, family, and marriage. The messages are strong and restrictive. Even people who think they have our best interests in mind will offer limiting opinions about life in general, let alone our dreams and possibilities. They accept good enough as their model of thinking and project that belief onto us.

2. Suppressive Cultures and Environments. Many cultures in our homes, schools, work settings, and communities are autocratic, bureaucratic, disrespectful, dishonest, and manipulative. To function in such environments, one must accept limiting regulations and policies, rigid and often irrational practices, and the narrow-minded people whose thinking create and foster such settings.

3. Pervasive Negative Media. Most media is often marked by disrespect, dishonesty, lewdness, and violence. Most television programs, movies, magazines, newspapers, and the Internet thrive on hooking our minds by appealing to the negative in life. When we fill our minds with negativity, we reinforce limited thinking and lower our self-expectations.

4. Our Own Unhealthy Lifestyles. This factor involves daily behavior that results in poor health and low stamina, which are significant obstacles in meeting the ongoing challenges of life effectively. We often justify these lifestyle results by citing how busy our lives are.

An Unconscious Expectation: Join The Crowd

These four forces are the limiters, the de-energizers, and the sources of de-motivation. They affect nearly everyone. They are ever-present influences that lessen the curiosity, creativity, and ambition of a creative, independent person and form the illusion that just surviving is an acceptable goal in life.

We lose the power of independent thinking when something outside of us influences our thinking, sensing, and acting and conditions us to respond without using our own reasoning. Over time, in many cases, our reactions become automatic.

We become convinced that it's easier to join the crowd rather than to stand alone, to survive rather than thrive. These limiting forces persist day after day, and we grow battle weary, physically, intellectually, and emotionally—and give in.

Then we get what we expect and accept, and it's only good enough.

Effect: The Impact of Good Enough Thinking

A mind conditioned by limitation produces thinking and actions that breed conformity and mediocrity. In general, you have little awareness of this impact and few skills to offset it and therefore you *unconsciously* live with:

1. A Loss of Independent Thinking
2. Lack of Purpose and a Tolerance for Unfulfilling Work
3. Static, Uninspiring Relationships
4. Poor Health, Addiction to Busyness, Work-Life Imbalance
5. Passivity, Inaction, and Failure to Risk

1. A Loss of Independent Thinking. With good enough as an unconscious mode of thinking, you think and believe within limits, confined by the status quo. Independent thinking is mostly silenced and you do not filter external opinions, beliefs, and advice through your own life experiences. You allow external voices to dominate your mind in several ways:

a) You respond automatically to many circumstances you encounter and often make poor decisions. Your reactions are based on previous experiences in the same or similar situations and you act without much reflection, resorting to the easier, conditioned response designed much of the time just to get by the circumstances you are facing. In many cases, this takes the form of misguided intuition (as described by Daniel Kahneman's System 1 in *Thinking Fast and Slow*). [4] While relying on intuition is effective at times, it leads to emotional decision making in situations that may need more self-reflection and conscious thought. This results in poor choices.

---

[4] Daniel Kahneman, *Thinking Fast and Slow*, (New York: Farrar, Straus, and Giroux, 2011), 19-44.

b) You begin to distrust your own experiences and wisdom, to lose confidence in yourself, and to give outside input much greater value than your own insights. This has two results: i) taking feedback too personally rather than trusting yourself to self-assess, learn, and develop, and ii) allowing yourself to be pressured, talked out of, or manipulated into decisions or outcomes that in your best thinking and decision making you would reject. Your own thinking, insights, views, and opinions are often silent when there are opposing group energies, beliefs, and actions.

Valuable time, effort, expenses, and, most importantly, personal honesty are lost when we side with the crowd rather than claiming and pursuing our unique perspectives. Under many circumstances, without much consideration, we agree with outside opinion and action. Under other circumstances, we consciously choose not to disagree. In either case, our actions represent the absence of independent, informed thinking and less than the best of ourselves. We follow the herd.

c) You become a pawn in the business of consumerism. Without independent thinking, you find yourself seduced by the next new thing or fad, accumulating things whether needed or not. Wants become needs and then control buying habits.

d) You allow policies and regulations to have priority over common sense. When good enough is a mindset, you are prone to rely strictly on a policy or regulation and often fail to argue for exceptions even where common sense calls for a better solution. When the power of independent thinking is lost, you are only capable of following directions from someone else, and, in spite of circumstances that require different solutions, your thinking and behavior become rigid and, many times, you overlook the obvious.

While examples of policy over common sense are ordinary, here's a story that illustrates blind policy adherence to the extreme.

General Joe Foss was a fighter pilot in World War II. He was fortunate to survive many life-threatening sorties and, in the Pacific campaign, shot down twenty-six enemy planes and was awarded the Congressional Medal of Honor by President Franklin Roosevelt. He served two terms as Governor of South Dakota. Late in his life, he was asked to speak at the U.S. Military Academy at West Point about his experiences leading to the Medal of Honor.

General Foss was eighty-six years old, had limited mobility, and used a wheel chair, so the Military Academy sent an Army Major to escort him to and from the Academy. As is the custom among Medal of Honor recipients, he wore the Medal of Honor around his neck as he entered an airport. The security personnel thought the Medal of Honor, which had a five-pointed star, might be used as a weapon of some kind. Although the military aide explained what the Medal of Honor was, no one on the staff understood its meaning. The security personnel insisted that General Foss surrender the Medal before boarding the plane. Understandably, he refused.

A security impasse followed. The security screeners were unable to make a decision and called their supervisor who also couldn't recognize the Medal and didn't accept the aide's further explanation. Again the supervisor requested General Foss leave the Medal. He refused again. A stalemate.

Finally, after the supervisor called his manager and discussed the matter at length, General Foss and the Congressional Medal of Honor were allowed to board the plane. Common sense prevailed and blind adherence to a policy was overturned. The need to confiscate a Congressional Medal of Honor from an eighty six year old retired general officer who was formerly Governor of South Dakota, and was escorted by a uniformed Army officer was finally understood to be without merit. [5]

---

[5] Paraphrased excerpt from editorial by Mike Rosen, (Denver Post, circa 2004).

2. Lack of Purpose and a Tolerance for Unfulfilling Work. A mind filled with ideas, beliefs, and opinions from other people cannot know itself. You have no way to discover your *raison d'etre*, your unique path to tap your potential. There is no internal driving force that lifts you to higher achievement.

Without a clear, compelling purpose larger than yourself, you are drawn to work for the wrong reasons. Seduced by money, benefits, ego, or power, or pressured by family and society, you overlook the intrinsic motivation of your deepest interests. You ignore your potential gifts and talents and develop only those abilities that are good enough to get by.

You fail to seek what could be a love of work, a passion, and a life of inspiration and, instead, settle for work lacking in purpose and enjoyment and only requiring either average effort or work that is done with effort but for the wrong reasons.

At some point in life, many people suddenly realize that their work is unfulfilling, having no inherent, added value for them and even for their customers or clients.

3. Static, Uninspiring Relationships. Settling for only good enough in life spreads into work, social, and family relationships and draws people of like mind. You unknowingly foster ongoing relationships that espouse good enough thinking. Most of these relationships remain static over time and do not develop into deeper, more meaningful human bonds.

In many situations, people engaging in dysfunctional behaviors of gossip, conflict, negativity, judgment, blaming, and criticism surround you. There are few models of healthy, meaningful relationships if good enough is merely the standard. Observing and experiencing negative and toxic relationships takes an emotional toll, saps energy, and reinforces limitation.

Lacking your own clear set of standards for your relationships combined with accepting all things good enough, you don't ask yourself if your relationships are positive, developing, and inspiring. Instead, you settle for whatever they are, accepting that an average or even dysfunctional relationship is better than none at all. Of course, in the reverse, you are equally responsible if you are average or dysfunctional with someone else. Generally, most people conveniently ignore how they are contributing to their relationships.

4. Poor Health due to An Addiction to Busyness and Work-Life Imbalance. With an absence of independent thinking and no clear, positive direction in life, we accept the concept of imbalance as a given. We settle for doing what we think is the best we can, given the circumstances, fostering the illusion of self-limitation even more.

So we develop an addiction to busyness. We commute unreasonably, overwork, and overlook relationship needs, particularly in our families. Most importantly, busyness results in insufficient time to take care of ourselves through daily exercise, healthy nutrition, and good sleep. We fail to nourish our mind, body, and spirit. We take our health for granted and our poor fitness condition quickly becomes an obstacle to our professional and personal potential.

An addiction to being busy, of over committing relative to the time and effort available, of losing a sense of how to meet both your personal and work needs, and missing many of life's rich moments---all are symptoms of the daily "can't get off the treadmill" lifestyle. Ellen Goodman, journalist and Pulitzer Prize winner, so aptly describes the quizzical rationale behind contradictory work-life actions, "Normal is getting dressed in clothes that you buy for work and driving through traffic in a car that you are still paying for---in order to get to the job you need to pay for the clothes and the car, and the house you leave vacant all day so you can afford to live in it." [6]

---

[6] Ellen Goodman. (n.d.). BrainyQuote.com. Retrieved February 27, 2015, from Brainy Quote.com Web site: http://www.brainyquote.com/quotes/quotes/e/ellengoodm137005.html

5. Passivity, Inaction, and Failure to Risk. This effect appears in two aspects of our behavior:

a) We fear failure. As children we risk many times a day and are mostly unaffected by failure. We fall and get up, over and over. We try any number of things and though we may not achieve, we continue to risk. As we age, failure forms a defensive shield against risking. Fear of failure and its resultant punishment or loss of esteem causes us to hold back when risking might be appropriate. So we decide that good enough applies in most of the situations where we previously tried something and failed or did less than we expected. Then we back off and create a smaller and smaller comfort zone of risk.

b) We avoid taking a stand. Since we rely so readily on others' opinions and approval, we do not have the confidence that comes from the strength of our own clear beliefs. As a result, even in seemingly minor situations, we avoid the risk of taking a stand. We play it safe, and generally react only when necessary.

A striking example of less than your best occurs when you ignore or consciously decide not to confront inappropriate, negative, or evil behavior, whether it's discrimination, bullying, or any act that dehumanizes. You decide not to risk getting involved, and always for a reason you believe is justified. At your best you wouldn't accept such behavior and would take action.

This type of thinking leads to Albert Einstein's powerful insight that "the world is a dangerous place, not because of those who do evil, but because of those who look on and do nothing."

Lest we forget …

First They Came

First they came for the communists, and I did not speak out--
because I was not a communist;
Then they came for the socialists, and I did not speak out--
because I was not a socialist;
Then they came for the trade unionists, and I did not speak out--
because I was not a trade unionist;
Then they came for the Jews, and I did not speak out--
because I was not a Jew;
Then they came for me--
and there was no one left to speak out for me.
Pastor Martin Niemölle [7]

---

[7] Martin Niemölle (1892–1984), 1946 WWII lecture, (a prominent Protestant pastor who emerged as an outspoken public foe of Adolf Hitler and spent the last seven years of Nazi rule in concentration camps), location unknown.

So Who Is Thinking for You? Have You Settled for Less?

There are two challenges to overcome in your thinking.

The first challenge is *not* people telling you that you are not good enough. The problem is people are telling you that you *are* good enough, that all you can be is good enough, yet you sense in your heart and mind that you have greater potential to learn more, do more, and be more. The message that other people are shouting loud and clear, over and over, is that you should settle for what *they* believe is good enough. And just in case you begin to see greater possibilities for yourself and express that to others, many people will immediately tell you why your ideas won't work and try to put you back in the box of good enough thinking.

The second challenge is that you are unknowingly prone to go along with them and accept their limited expectations of you. So the expectation of being only adequate then becomes your own and you buy into the *illusion of good enough*.

This phenomenon is explained in part by Herbert Simon's theory of bounded rationality. Simon concluded that people generally do not seek to optimize their decision making since there is too much information and mental work to consider everything. As Simon described, people have cognitive limits when processing all the information involved in making decisions. Hence, they will sacrifice trying to optimize their decisions and will seek decisions that are satisfactory or good enough. Simon termed this *satisficing*. [8]

---

[8] Herbert Simon, *The Economist*, March 20, 2009.

The theory of bounded rationality describes an important element of human behavior. It is a learned limitation, a conditioned response. You are not born with the limiting nature of satisficing. It occurs primarily as a result of unconscious conditioning thereby creating the powerful obstacle that

your mind does not know that it does not know.

You develop a blind spot, an illusion, as to what's possible for yourself, for others, and for society, defending your limited beliefs and arguing their validity. You think and speak like the crowd, stuck in and unaware of your self-limitations.

When you settle for good enough as your standard self-belief, your independent thinking and inner voice of reason are quieted. Interestingly, you periodically awaken and ask yourself if that is all there is to life, Alfie? Unfortunately, you normally respond to that question by quickly returning to spending excessive time and effort on trivial and routine matters just to keep yourself busy and feel adequate.

You blindly resort to good enough thinking and rejoin the masses.

III

Choices of Your Mind

Mind is the master power that molds and makes,
And we are Mind, and evermore we take,
The tool of thought, and shaping what we will,
Bring forth a thousand joys, a thousand ills.
We think in secret and it comes to pass.
Environment is but our looking glass.
James Allen

The Mind Rules

Our thoughts and beliefs project energy onto everyone and everything we encounter and that energy attracts most of what appears in our lives. Whether positive or negative, our thoughts are magnets and draw to us what we think about and focus our attention on.

Mind defines. Mind creates. Mind rules.

Our minds shape beliefs, form thoughts, make decisions, and take actions and life develops accordingly. Understanding the cause and effect relationship between what's on your mind, what you attract, and how you act is the initial step in confronting the illusion of good enough and tapping into greater possibilities for yourself and for others.

A Range of Thinking

An initial step in understanding greater possibilities in thinking and performance is to consider a range of mindsets that produce different levels of performance. Our research projects identified participant mindsets and respective performance levels in three categories (Negative, Good Enough, Excellent) and seven specific mindsets (Destruct, Decay, Survival, Frenetic, Development, Craft, and Artistry) within those categories. [9]

---

[9] Randall P. Kunkel, Principal Researcher, *The Performance-Productivity Study*: 342 participants from IBM, Pennsylvania Power & Light, The Eisenhower Medical Center, State Farm Insurance, and select secondary schools, 1980-85, and *The Mindset-Performance Study*: 364 participants from The Cooper Aerobics Center, Kaiser Permanente, Hewlett Packard, Digital Equipment Corporation, and select K-12 school systems in Colorado, 1985-91.

Mindsets of Negativity

Two types of mindsets produce negative behavior: *destruct* and *decay*. A person with a destructive mindset feels like a victim of circumstances. This individual finds fault, blames others, creates conflict, and is unconcerned with the negative effect on others. A person with the mindset of decay, while also feeling like a victim, is detached, and avoids interaction and potential conflict with others.

The mindsets of destruct and decay create emotional tension, high stress, toxic relationships, poor performance, and a loss of productivity not only in the individuals who harbor these mindsets but also in persons who interact with them.

Mindsets of Good Enough

Survival and *frenetic* are the mindsets that define good enough thinking. An individual with survival thinking seeks the path of minimum requirements. A person with frenetic thinking shows some initiative and energy but is scattered in multiple directions with little follow-through.

Individuals with survival and frenetic mindsets rely primarily on outside directions, create average and mediocre results, focus on the status quo, and seldom embrace change. If allowed to exist for a period of time, the belief of good enough becomes engrained and achievement is seen as unnecessary or too difficult. Consider why students with good enough thinking accept the guaranteed B without having to take the final exam rather than taking the exam and trying for the A. The added time and effort to study for the final is seen as unnecessary since a B is good enough in their opinion.

Survival and frenetic mindsets are obstacles to learning and achievement. They block us from tapping our true potential by implying that outside factors are the cause of our limited performance. And, unconsciously, we then have excuses that conveniently appear throughout our life experiences.

Mindsets of Excellence

People with mindsets of *development*, *craft*, and *artistry* produce thoughts and actions that result in high performance, productivity, and achievement. An individual with development thinking emphasizes learning and skill building. A person with the mindset of craft uses talents and discipline that produce advanced skills, high reliability, and quality. A key motivation of craft thinking is pride of work and a sense of contributing to a larger purpose. Someone with an artistry mindset has the qualities of craft as well as the added element of creativity under varying conditions. Artistry thinking results in sustained achievement through a combination of creative problem solving, effective decision making, a willingness to take risks, and persistence through obstacles.

As compared with the good enough student who accepts a B, the student committed to excellence uses development, craft, or artistry mindsets and will not necessarily be satisfied even with an A. This student thrives on inquiry and learning, not on the grade, and will pursue additional assignments or tasks that will result in added learning regardless of the time and effort involved.

Mindsets and Performance

Our performance research studies reveal the following percentage of people within these individual mindsets. [10]

MINDSETS PRODUCE PERFORMANCE

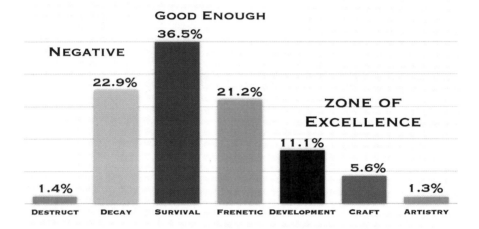

When we are young, we live on the right side of the chart, in excellence, thoroughly enjoying learning, growth, and achievement. As we get older we are conditioned toward the left categories of good enough and negativity. Limitation influences are much stronger than most of us realize. Unknowingly, many individuals settle into survival or frenetic and accept that this as a way of life. And, if there are significantly negative influences, some people develop thoughts and beliefs defined by decay and destruct.

Note the percentage of individuals in the good enough category totals nearly 58%. When adding the negativity category (24.3%), the percentage of people with low or no productivity totals approximately 82%. Since sustained productivity is a result of development, craft, and artistry mindsets, only 18% of the study participants contributed to achievement on a continuing basis.

[10] Randall P. Kunkel, Principal Researcher, *The Performance Distribution Study*: 1688 participants from Kaiser Permanente, Newman and Associates, GMACCM, GMACCM Healthcare, U.S. Air Force Academy, and select university athletic coaches and teams, 1992 – present.

Corporate Feedback

I have presented this chart model and data as part of speaking engagements, lectures, seminars, and consultations to over 32,000 business executives and managers, health care staff, coaches, and athletes across the country. In each presentation, I ask the audience if the distribution results seem valid based on their professional experiences.

The consensus feedback I have received is from executives and managers who reflected on their own internal organizational bureaucracies and felt that the percentages in the good enough category (survival and frenetic) were higher in their organizations than in the research results indicated. They added that their continuing challenge was to find individuals who rejected the good enough philosophy and were deeply committed to excellence.

Your Learning Depends on Your Mindset

A colleague of mine is a university professor in California. This past semester she taught a course that was part of a graduate program in leadership studies. After the students turned in the initial writing assignment, she was both elated and disappointed at the quality of writing. Several students clearly spent significant time and effort and their papers were excellent. A handful of papers, however, were below par. She took a few minutes and addressed the situation by explaining that accepting good enough as a measure of performance was below her expectations and, she surmised, below the expectations of each of the students. There was extended silence.

After the semester ended and students turned in their course evaluations, there were two student comments that stood out regarding the professor's expectations. One student said, "I thought you were talking directly to me. All your comments applied and I appreciate being made aware that good enough does not represent my best. Thank you for the valuable insights." Another student wrote, "How dare you imply that my work was only good enough and not my best. Your comments are not helpful."

Again, mind rules. You create results in your life relative to your thoughts, beliefs, and actions. And the mindset you choose on a day-to-day basis will create results that come from how you think, believe, and subsequently act. In short, you get what you expect.

Over these many years of researching human achievement, it is my experience that nearly all of us have the potential to achieve excellence in one of more aspects of our lives. The realization of that potential depends on what is on our mind, specifically the nature of thoughts and beliefs that shape our self-awareness toward development, craft, and artistry or toward frenetic, survival, decay, and destruct. Are we inspired to learn, achieve, and grow or are we conditioned with so many limitations that we settle for mediocrity and even argue against constructive feedback, learning, and improvement?

IV

The Catalysts of Inspiration

The Pursuit of Development, Craft, and Artistry

Success isn't a result of spontaneous combustion.
You must set yourself on fire.
Arnold Glasow

Dreams and hopes are starting points for human achievement. They open the mind and build the excitement. However, they alone do not create results. There must be a game plan, a clear path in mind, and then *action* to realize those dreams.

Most people dream about achievement. They talk much of the time about an idea they have, about something they would like to do. However it seems they don't get around to doing those things nearly as often as they wish. They dream. They don't take action. And good enough prevails.

To continually pursue new bests in all endeavors, you must find your own answer to this question:

What are the *major influences* and *critical actions* that will offset conforming to good enough and instead inspire me to development, craft, and artistry in work and life?

Research Focus

This question led me to focus my research on the behavior and habits of individuals with mindsets in development, craft, and artistry. These achievers are different in thought, belief, and action from nearly everyone else. They have an enhanced self-awareness and well-developed skill sets that sustain high levels of achievement at work and home most of the time. They are consistently committed to learning and taking risks outside their comfort zone.

While they admit to losing the focus on excellence at times, and even experiencing good enough and negative thinking under some challenging circumstances, they quickly rebound to what they term their *pursuit of their best.*

The key is their commitment and persistence to constant self-assessment and improvement. At every opportunity, they seek to learn, develop, and become more effective at whatever they are doing, to tap a greater potential within themselves.

While diverse in skills, personality, age, and experience, they have a consensus response to what they say are the key actions that contribute the most to their continued, high achievement. Our research is clear. They pursue the mindsets of development, craft, and artistry by using four *catalysts of inspiration:*

1. A Strong, Unconventional, Independent Mind

2. A Circle of Exemplary Relationships

3. Highly Developed Gifts and Talents

4. Excellent Health and Fitness

These four catalysts get to the core of achievement and effectiveness by influencing the power of thought, belief, and action. Again, the mind rules by causing behavioral change.

Much has been studied and written about how to increase productivity, perform at high levels, achieve consistently, and be successful. Often cited examples include purpose, goal setting, career and life planning, core competencies, collaboration, teamwork, time management, and technology. While each of these has some benefit for most anyone, they generally produce only incremental changes in behavior since they are supplemental and secondary to the importance of the changing of mindset, the altering of thoughts and beliefs.

The catalysts of inspiration form a solid foundation for many of these secondary factors to be more effective by opening the mind to possibility, building human support and reinforcement, and developing unique skills and competencies all within a context of body-mind-spirit health and fitness.

Catalyst 1

Cultivate A Strong, Independent Mind

Think Unconventionally

An Independent Mind Is Hungry and Thinks Differently

Creativity is the foundation for freedom of mind and spirit. A development, craft, or artistry mindset constantly strengthens an open, inquiring mind by rediscovering imagination and the power of possibilities.

Most people use default, restricted thinking that has been shaped all their lives. They respond automatically based on ways they previously were conditioned to handle situations.

Individuals with mindsets of excellence have replaced that old default of automatic response with a new thought process that consistently has them envisioning all types of options in situations they encounter. They develop their independent minds through:

    a. Pushing the Envelope to Pursue Possibilities

    b. Understanding that Nothing has Meaning Until ...

    c. Embracing The Power of Optimism

    d. Using A Language of Excellence

a. Pushing the envelope to pursue possibilities. A mindset of excellence envisions and initially considers alternatives without limitation, outside the norm of average thought. This creative thinking is an anomaly, an exception, a rarity that sets the mind free to pursue possibilities in all situations.

b. Understanding that nothing has meaning until we decide what that meaning is. Life is perhaps 5% (or less) what happens to us and 95% (or more) how we interpret and respond to what is happening. It is our interpretation of external events that gives them meaning. Situations and circumstances are neutral until we decide what they mean whether positive, negative, or insignificant. Individuals in the excellence category refuse to accept the limiting biases and judgments of others. They make their own interpretations, and decide accordingly.

There is an often-noted parable about a shoe factory that sends two marketing scouts to a distant country to study the possibilities of expanding the shoe business. The first scout sends back a message that the situation is hopeless, no one wears shoes, and there is no market. The other scout responds enthusiastically that this is an outstanding business opportunity since no one has shoes.[11] In any situation, the meaning we give to the circumstances determines what we see and how we think and act.

c. Being optimistic. Optimism frees thinking to see positive outcomes and pursue achievement. By its very nature, pessimism results in limitation. When difficult challenges arise or setbacks occur, optimism gives hope and encouragement.

Whether in business, sports, health, or other life situations, individuals and teams with optimistic thinking will consistently achieve more, particularly under stressful conditions when creative options are needed. Sustained optimism builds momentum and has increasingly positive impact over time.

---

[11] As described by Rosamund Stone Zander & Benjamin Zander, *The Art of Possibility*, 9.

d. Using the language of achievement and excellence. There is a vocabulary of excellence among the high achievers that includes specific words and phrases that influence beliefs, thoughts, and actions toward possibility and achievement. These words shift the focus of thinking, communication, and action from limitation, survival, and negativity to positive thought, hope, and energy. These words are influential cues in leadership, coaching, counseling, and social interactions:

yes	optimistic	upward	tremendous
excellent	superb	farther	affirmative
helpful	encouraging	beyond	OK
inspirational	enhance	constructive	artistic
promising	hopeful	creative	opportunity
imaginative	inventive	better	well
quality	terrific	outstanding	well done
exciting	energetic	powerful	brilliant
why not?	awesome	be bold	go for it

Reflections on an Independent Mind

At any point in your life, you experience the accumulated effects of all the choices you have ever made prior to then. How you think and act today is a reflection of all the thinking and decisions you have made in the past. If you choose to change your thinking, you can then change your actions. By unlocking your conditioned mind and considering fresh thoughts and ideas, you can see possibilities that previously were hidden.

An independent mind sometimes needs to be a little crazy, off the wall, far out. It requires thinking freely. It taps into that state of possibility thinking that we were born with and is the source of creative problem solving within our personal and professional lifestyles.

Loosen up a bit.

Catalyst 2

Surround Yourself with Exemplary Relationships

Create An Extraordinary Team of Integrity and Excellence

The sole purpose of human existence
is to kindle a light in the darkness of mere being.
Dr. Carl Gustav Jung

Exemplary Relationships

To consistently tap their best, the highest achievers in my research rely upon a *team of excellence* comprised of *exemplary individuals* with integrity, character, and authenticity.

These achievers refuse to settle for good enough and, with exemplary people influencing, challenging, and encouraging them throughout their lives, are unstoppable in their search for learning, growth and achievement in life. Their powerful team has three key types of relationships:

- A Steadfast Life Partner

- A Select Few Trusted Friends and Colleagues

- Respected, Learned Mentors

Create An Extraordinary Team

The most important, influential, and inspirational source is your *steadfast life partner*, who contributes immensely to your compelling purpose and goals and is by your side through all of life's challenges. The choice of a partner is one of the most important decisions anyone makes in life. Life partners inspire one another and lift each other's spirit.

Second, you need a select few *trusted friends and colleagues* who you can count on under all circumstances. These are relationships based on mutual dedication to integrity, high character, and excellence in work and personal life. You are in each other's corner at all times.

Third, you need *respected, learned mentors* whose belief systems, insights, and skills stimulate your mind. These are outstanding people who believe in you and have the experience and competencies that will guide you to become more effective both professionally and personally. These mentors are master teachers, perhaps a Yoda, a Gandalf, a Mister Miyagi, someone who inspires you to achieve more than you would do alone. They are there to advise, challenge, and encourage independent thinking and beliefs to help you realize your possibilities.

Nourishing, and inspiring describe the nature of *all* relationships on any team of excellence. To achieve this, ask some key questions and make some hard choices.

"Is this person lifting my spirits and energizing me?"

"Does he express consistent possibility thinking?"

"Does this individual stimulate my thinking and learning?"

"Am I a better person because of his influence?"

"Does this person bring out my best?"

Questions we ask about ourselves are sometimes more difficult.

"Am I lifting the spirits of those around me?

"Are my attitude and actions positive and energizing?"

"Am I contributing to the quality of life of others?"

"Does my presence make a positive difference?"

"Do I inspire those around me?"

Integrity and Character

Integrity is the primary foundation of exemplary, inspirational relationships. It is the basis for self-leadership and a positive influence on others.

Integrity includes a number of human qualities: honesty, respect, dignity, ethical actions, and a moral code that empowers and inspires self and others. It simply means being true to the *absolute best* of yourself and honest with others. Integrity appears in all life roles: spouse, parent, friend, colleague, and coach. It influences you to choose the harder right instead of the easier good enough, regardless of the circumstances.

A person's integrity breeds character and character leads to trusting that person's thinking, decisions, and actions. You project your integrity and character at all times with an impact on all relationships, whether family, business, or social.

Family, relatives, friends, associates, even casual acquaintances are always learning from you and you become what you practice. And it's what you do in those frequent, trivial situations that are the building blocks for strong character that is necessary to handle more challenging situations. You must practice making character-based decisions as you practice any other skill.

Take A Stand

A distinctive action of individuals with integrity and character is to take a stand to support, encourage, and help others in various life situations. This occurs most importantly in the face of injustice, inequality, falsehood, or manipulation. Make those difficult decisions, such as holding to an unpopular opinion, confronting potential harmful actions, and standing up for those unable to defend themselves. In the midst of World War II, Winston Churchill made an interesting point by saying "You have enemies? Good. That means you've stood up for something in your life."

Each time an individual takes a stand, he becomes an influence on others to listen, consider, and possibly take action. In June of 1966, Senator Robert F. Kennedy went to South Africa to confront apartheid. At the University of Cape Town, he spoke to a crowd of anti-apartheid students and said, "Each time a man stands up for an ideal or acts to improve the lot of others or strikes out against injustice, he sends forth a tiny ripple of hope; and crossing each other from a million different centers of energy and daring, those ripples build a current which can sweep down the mightiest walls of oppression and resistance." [12]

[12] Robert F. Kennedy, "Ripple of Hope Speech", University of Cape Town, June, 1966.

Taking A Stand When Only You Know Something Is Wrong

At a Volvo Masters tennis tournament in 1982, Vitas Gerulaitis and Eliot Teltscher met in the semifinals. They split the first two sets, with the intensity and level of play increasing with each game. It was the eighth game when Gerulaitis fought his way to match point.

Both players stayed in the backcourt for a number of shots until, sensing an opportunity, Gerulaitis took the net. Teltscher hit a lob. Gerulaitis attacked again. Teltscher hit a powerful cross-court shot. Gerulaitis stretched and tipped the ball. It hit the net cord, and fell over. Somehow, Teltscher charged the net, dove and managed to lift the ball over Gerulaitis's head. Gerulaitis, clearly amazed at Teltscher's athleticism to get to the ball, was out of position, and hit his return wide.

The cheers and applause were deafening. After such a long rally with numerous difficult shots, Teltscher had taken the point and was back in the match. However, Teltscher stood by the net and indicated to the umpire that he had touched the net when he stretched for the ball.

The crowd was stunned. No one, the umpire included, had seen any violation. There was a lot at stake: money, rankings, endorsements, and TV interviews. None of that mattered for Eliot Teltscher. What mattered was his moral code. He shook Gerulaitis's hand, waved to the crowd, thanking them for their support, and walked off the court. [13]

---

[13] Author unknown, Paraphrased from article (New York Times, March, 1982).

Reflections on Exemplary Relationships

Nourishing, inspiring people bring consistent energy, excitement, and growth to all they encounter. They create a positive ripple effect. When joined by others of a similar nature, the team becomes synergistic, achieving far more together than the sum of their individual efforts.

If you want to tap your deepest capabilities, you need to be an integral member of a team of exemplary relationships, to have and to be an inspirational partner, a dear friend, a trusted colleague, and a learned mentor. Create, nurture, learn from, and influence an extraordinary team of exemplary relationships, a team of integrity and excellence.

Catalyst 3

Extensively Develop Your Gifts and Talents

Mine Your Diamonds

But yield who will to their separation,
My object in living is to unite
My avocation with my vocation
As my two eyes make one in sight.
Only where love and need are one,
And the work is play for mortal stakes,
Is the deed ever really done
For heaven and the future's sakes.
Robert Frost, *Two Tramps in Mudtime*

Gifted Intelligences

Every person is a diamond in the rough, a particular blend of inherent gifts and talents. Harvard psychologist Howard Gardner offers a set of categories that he developed from his research on *gifted intelligences.* [14]

Intelligence	Focus
Linguistic	auditory, speaking, writing, reading
Logical-Mathematical	structure, numbers, rationale
Visual-Spatial	art, architecture, design, photography
Bodily-Kinesthetic	sports, hands-on work, movement
Musical	performing arts, rhythm, harmony
Interpersonal	relationships, people skills, teamwork
Intrapersonal	self, introspection, independence
Naturalist	plants, animals, nature sensitivity
Existential	life, death, ultimate realities

---

[14] Howard Gardner, *Frames of Mind*, (New York: Basic Books, 1985), pp. 73-76.

In addition, from my research, there are other natural categories that could describe your gifts and talents:

Digital	computers, electronics, communications
Behavioral	motivation, achievement, group dynamics
Visionary	possibility, big picture, future orientation
Entrepreneurial	business, effectiveness, leverage
Process-oriented	*how* something is happening (not *what*)

Several of these areas of intelligence apply to you. It's how you are custom-designed, unique and special. It's a predisposition, a strong natural orientation that inspires you.

Is it music, or sports, or literature, or computers, or some other area? Perhaps you love the performing arts, or are fascinated by multimedia and are excellent with numbers so you might consider having your own film production company. Or you enjoy sports and are drawn to helping people and would enjoy coaching or physical therapy.

Whatever the focus, your gifts are uplifting to yourself and to others. Whatever may be your combination, you have a natural capacity to understand, learn, and use those intelligences to contribute in ways that express your best.

Love What You Do, Do What You Love

By focusing on what resonates for you, what you are naturally drawn to, and what is your calling, you have the opportunity to create a life in which you love what you do and do what you love.

It is of critical importance to align work and play "as my two eyes make one in sight" if you are to optimize opportunities to make a difference in your life.

Your work is going to fill a large part of your life,
and the only way to be truly satisfied
is to do what you believe is great work.
And the only way to do great work is to love what you do.
If you haven't found it yet, keep looking.
Don't settle.

As with all matters of the heart,
you'll know when you find it.
And, like any great relationship,
it just gets better and better as the years roll on.

So keep looking until you find it.
Don't settle. [15]

---

[15] Steven Jobs, Commencement Address, Stanford University, 2005.

Thinking You're Not Gifted Is Settling for Good Enough

I have observed many people who discount their abilities. "I'm not creative," "I could never do math well," or "I don't have an ear for language." These are classic beliefs that come from accepting what others have said and then not pursuing further discovery and learning in those areas. Discounting your potential in any way carries a strong message that you're limited and that self-belief spills over into how you view yourself overall. What these beliefs do not address is that a dedicated focus on learning, lots of hard work, and persistence will consistently result in improvement. Your abilities are ultimately dependent on your belief in yourself and your commitment to pursue learning. Do not allow anyone to define your capabilities and potential.

Misty Copeland had every reason to settle for good enough. Her single mom raised her with 5 siblings, barely supporting the family. They lived month to month in a motel in San Pedro, California. Misty had a love of ballet. However, as she entered her teen years, her body did not align with the classical ballet physique. She was told by many in the ballet community that her body was a distraction. In addition, she was not Caucasian and she understood that the ballet society wasn't keen on having a brown face in such a white world.

Misty sensed her own abilities and faced the challenges, refusing to accept what so many others said. After years of intense training, practice, and learning, she achieved what others thought was not possible. She is only the second African-American woman to gain the level of soloist in the American Ballet Theatre, and the first ever to play the "Firebird." In June 2015, Misty was promoted to principal dancer of the American Ballet Theatre, the first female African-American dancer to reach that status in the 75-year history of the company.

Misty is the national ambassador for the Boys and Girls Club of America. Her personal mission is to help other young ballet enthusiasts break through the limitations of traditional ballet and live their dreams.[16]

---

[16] Misty Copeland, *Life in Motion: An Unlikely Ballerina* (New York: Touchstone, 2014).

A Path With a Purpose

Purpose is the place
where your deep gladness meets the world's needs.
Frederick Buechner

A clear, positive direction of where you are going is a blueprint for a successful present and future. You must discover a calling that involves work that is larger and more important than yourself. To achieve your best in life and work, you need the inspiration that a path with a *compelling purpose* gives you.

Within your gifted intelligences and talents lies your purpose in life. A compelling purpose embodies deep personal values and serves as a constant compass. It keeps you on track to spend your time and effort on actions that use your gifts, talents, and strengths to excel and make a difference. As Nietzsche so simply clarified, "He who has a *why* to live for can bear with almost any *how*."

Here's an example of a youngster who found his purpose early in life. The Ryan's Well Foundation (http://www.ryanswell.ca) delivers safe water and sanitation to small villages in Africa. These efforts grew from the commitment of one boy, Ryan Hreljac, who, in his 1st grade class, learned of the pressing need for clean and safe water in developing countries. With the support of family, friends, and the community, Ryan raised enough money to drill a well in Africa. In 1999, at age seven, Ryan's first well was placed at Angolo Primary School in northern Uganda. To this day, the well continues to serve the community. Ryan started raising money for water projects in 1998. His Foundation was formed in 2001. Since then, Ryan's Well has helped develop over 880 water projects and 1120 latrines bringing safe water and improved sanitation to over 824,000 people.

Another example of finding a calling is the experience of Susan Sygall. While studying to work with people with disabilities, Susan, at the age of 18, was involved in a car accident and became dependent on a wheelchair. This life-changing experience clarified her purpose as she committed her life to helping people with disabilities. Ms. Sygall is CEO and co-founder of Mobility International USA, and serves as a trainer, presenter and consultant throughout the United States, Latin America, Europe and Asia on leadership, international exchange, inclusion, and services for people with disabilities. She has conducted leadership trainings with people with disabilities, educators and policy makers in Vietnam, Micronesia, Bosnia, Brazil and Mexico. Ms. Sygall received a MacArthur Foundation Fellowship in 2000. [17]

The scope of a compelling purpose is clarified by Wes Jackson, Founder of The Land Institute and another MacArthur Foundation Fellow, with his claim, "If you think you're going to complete your life's work in your lifetime, you're not thinking big enough". [18]

---

[17] Susan Sygall and Ken Spillman, *No Ordinary Days* (Eugene, OR: New Hebrides Press, 2014).

[18] Wes Jackson, Interview in Salina, Kansas by Leslie A. Hennessy, Doctoral Dissertation, University of San Diego, 2014.

Continual Learning, Hard Work, Practice, Practice, Practice

The degree to which your gifts and strengths are developed depends on your genetics, outside influences, and the choices that you make during your life. You have considerable control over how you choose to spend your time and with whom. It takes a significant commitment of time, effort, and energy to develop your strengths to sustain the pursuit of your best.

To consistently perform at your best requires an unwavering curiosity to know the depth of your gifts and how to perfect them. The pursuit of best is a 24/7 endeavor that depends on your commitment to your true potential. You must challenge your mind-body-spirit to develop, learn, and use significantly more of your human abilities. You must devote extensive time and effort to recognizing your habits, stretching your comfort zones, and doing so with absolute dedication.

And then, of course, practice, practice, practice.

If I don't practice piano one day, I know it;
If I fail to practice two days in a row, my family knows,
and if I don't three days in a row, the public knows.
Arthur Rubenstein

The Good Enough Plateau

While there is benefit to a brief period of rest after significant effort, it is important to be careful of lingering and losing the momentum of achievement. There is a human tendency to settle into a comfort zone that could be the beginning of a return to good enough. We need to sense when we're not getting better at some skill or when it seems that doing the task is automatic. We have to consciously challenge ourselves, expand our comfort zone, and continue to pursue the next level of achievement in knowledge, skills, and capability.

It is ironic that, at a time in life when we are most skilled and experienced, most of us choose to retire, based on age alone. For a few, this retirement offers an opportunity to transition into volunteer service and they continue to apply their skills and knowledge. For many people, however, retirement is an acceptance of something less than what they know they are capable of and the beginning of a life less lived.

Sustained life achievement requires us to reject the good enough plateau, particularly the concept of retirement as society defines it, and to keep serving and contributing, to keep pursuing our best at all ages.

Creativity, Risk, Trial and Learning

We are born with an instinct for creativity. Most of our learning moments occur when we discover, solve, have insights, and grow. Our unconscious minds are consistently probing, making disparate connections, and feeding us new ways to see and handle our life experiences. Creativity leads to inspiration, risking, action, and learning.

I often hear the term *trial and error*. I don't believe there is trial and error or failure. Attempts to do anything bring opportunities to understand or learn something new. Discovery and learning occur even if a mistake is made. Mistakes, often termed failures by someone with a good enough mentality, can breed greater understanding and subsequent success at whatever is being tried. Edison described his continual light bulb experiments by saying he had not failed, but rather had discovered a thousand ways that would not work.

A more productive way of evaluating risk is to understand that there is no trial and error, only trial and *learning*. Trial and learning at every opportunity is critical. Risking unleashes your intellectual curiosity to read, discuss, observe, listen, and seek new information, fresh ideas, and contrary opinions. Constant creative trial and learning helps us discover added possibilities for the use of our gifts and talents. Albert Einstein is said to have claimed that he had no special talents, rather that he only was passionately curious.

Trial and Learning Through Risking and Almost

During the 2014 Boston Marathon Shalane Flanagan, one of the premier runners from the United States and a 2008 Olympic medalist, took an early lead and maintained a torrid pace. Ahead of the Boston record at the halfway point, she refused to back off and continued to lead a pack of seven runners from Kenya and Ethiopia, all of whom had better previous marathon times.

At the 19-mile mark the other runners gradually pulled ahead, continuing to maintain the challenging pace that Shalane had set. Ultimately, three of the runners broke the Boston course record and Shalane finished seventh, breaking her own personal record for the marathon by over 2 minutes.

Reflecting on the race during a television news interview, Shalane exclaimed, "I ran to win." While winning was not hers on that day, she was ecstatic with her performance. In the news conference after the race, she said, "I don't wish it were easier. I just wish I were better. It was really a heartfelt performance today." She immediately said she was looking forward to next year's marathon. She said, "I can say right now, I'll be back here until I win it."

This is the power of almost being successful, nearly mastering a skill, and coming close to a goal. Going for it and almost achieving anything inspires us to continue the journey, work even harder, and put in more effort.

Almost gives us added confidence that achievement is possible.

Share Your Gifts: Your Passion Inspires Others

You have your own gifts, your specific blend of intelligences. Your unique mixture of natural strengths is the basis of your artistry, your calling. It's the source of motivation, higher energy and persistence. In developing your gifts and talents, you become more qualified and valuable in work and life situations. You stand out as someone who is dedicated and loves what you do and has spent time and effort developing distinct skills. You have a way about you that exudes a deeper understanding of yourself, your capabilities, and how you can serve. Others deeply appreciate and are inspired by your commitment to excellence.

The following letter is from a foreign diplomat who was often at odds with U.S. policies. While visiting the U.S. Embassy in his own country, he was inspired by the attitude and actions of a single person's dedication to excellence and wrote this letter to his home ministry:

> During one of the past few days, I had occasion to visit the U.S. Embassy in our capital after official working hours. I arrived at a quarter to six and was met by the Marine on guard at the entrance of the Chancery. He asked if I would mind waiting while he lowered the two American flags at the Embassy.
>
> The Marine was dressed in a uniform which was spotless and neat; he walked with a measured tread from the entrance of the Chancery to the stainless steel flagpole before the Embassy and, almost reverently, lowered the flag to the level of his reach where he began to fold it in military fashion. He then released the flag from the clasps attaching it to the rope, stepped back from the pole, made an about face, and carried the flag between his hands, one above, one below, and placed it securely on a stand before the Chancery. He then marched over to the second flagpole and repeated the same lonesome ceremony.

On the way between poles, he mentioned to me very briefly that he would soon be finished. After completing his task, he apologized for the delay out of pure courtesy, as nothing less than incapacity would have prevented him from fulfilling his goal, and said to me, "Thank you for waiting, Sir, I had to pay honor to my country."

I have had to tell this story because there was something impressive about a lone Marine carrying out a ceremonial task which obviously meant very much to him and which, in its simplicity made the might, the power, and the glory of the United States of America stand forth in a way that a mighty wave of military aircraft, or the passage of a super-carrier, or a parade of 10,000 men could never have made manifest. [19]

When Excellence *Must* Be Achieved, Passion Appears

Excellence in life actions appears in one of two situations. Either you love whatever it is you're doing or what you're doing has such paramount importance for you or someone else that it must be done and done as well as possible given the circumstances. In the latter case, the importance overrides whether you like the task.

Perhaps it's a life-saving situation, or an emergency where time is a factor, or something that will make a significant difference in someone else's life. Whatever the reason, the added dimension of passion to get the job done is present and inspiring to all concerned.

---

[19] O. E. Sanchez, *The Scout*, August 5, 2009.

Your Best Is *Not* Necessarily Perfection

Doing our best, that is, excellence, even artistry in its most pure form, shouldn't be confused with trying to be perfect. In fact, perfection is often the enemy of best. Discovering your next best in any endeavor is a commitment to continued learning and growing in the pursuit of achievement. Pursuit is a journey, an on-going experience of risking, learning, and growing over and over again, a lifelong dedication to discovering your true potential.

Over the course of my research projects, I have asked a number of individuals to comment on perfection. Perhaps the clearest understanding comes from Steve Sinton and John Quinlan, California ranchers and winegrowers from Paso Robles. In their unpredictable professions, they face a myriad of daily challenges to keep their businesses successful. Their creativity, decision making, and actions over the past 5 decades are the epitome of sustained achievement. In discussing perfection at the 2014 CA Ranchers' Forum, Steve and John gave the following insights, "Doing your best always needs to be in context---how much time do you have available for the task, what other priorities exist for you and whether there is a goal that can be achieved after which additional effort doesn't offer anything. Perfection can be an impossible standard that actually fosters 'good enough' because you fear you will not be able to achieve perfection. Your best is seldom going to be perfect. Doing your best should inherently have an improvement component on previous efforts, so it almost by definition isn't perfection." [20]

---

[20] Steve Sinton and John Quinlan, Camatta Creek Ranchers' Forum, Canyon Ranch, CA, June, 2014.

Reflections on Gifts and Talents

The ultimate in work and life is to do what you love to do in the presence of people who are enamored by your gifts and talents. It is those professional and personal environments and circumstances where you can fully express your skills and passion, have the freedom to exercise highly creative thinking, make important decisions, and be responsible for results. It is there you will make your greatest contributions and find consistent encouragement to learn and grow.

And it doesn't matter what your endeavor is. Passion emanates from you when you tap your gifts and talents. Your energy is high. Your excitement is apparent. Your way of being inspires others. You are pursuing artistry, and that can be in any field or profession.

We must learn to honor excellence
in every socially-accepted human activity,
And to scorn shoddiness, however exalted the activity.
An excellent plumber is infinitely more admirable
than an incompetent philosopher.
The society which scorns excellence in plumbing
because plumbing is a humble activity
and tolerates shoddiness in philosophy
because philosophy is an exalted activity
will have neither good plumbing nor good philosophy.
Neither its pipes nor its theories will hold water. [21]

---

[21] John Gardner, *Excellence*, (W.W. Norton & Company, 1961) 101-102.

Catalyst 4

Optimize Health and Fitness

Heal Thyself

This catalyst is critical, paramount, imperative, life-giving. Emerson said it simply, "The first wealth is health." Nothing is more important to our motivation, performance, and achievement than our health. Nothing.

Our health and fitness must be excellent if we are to optimize performance and achievement throughout every area of our lives, benefitting ourselves and all family, friends, and colleagues. How can we possibly tap our best in any area of our lives unless we are of sound and fit mind, body, and spirit? The challenges and demands of our lifestyles can only be met and handled well if we are at our best physically, emotionally, and spiritually.

The irony of health and fitness is that it is easy to intellectually understand and, more times than not, difficult to act upon. There is a strong tendency to take our overall health for granted. We minimize our efforts to challenge ourselves with physical exercise, nutritional awareness, and spiritual development. We take the easier road in our daily lives, seeking comfortable rather than active lifestyles.

Yet, to achieve excellence, our physical self must be constantly challenged at whatever level is necessary to benefit us. For with excellent health, we respond to life challenges with significantly greater energy and stamina. Our daily experience is more vigorous and satisfying. Our attitude is more positive and influential.

With poor or even average health, our options are more limited since we lack one or more aspects of physical, mental, emotional, or spiritual strength.

Excellent health is the basis for the successful application of each of the other catalysts of inspiration. Health in body, mind, and spirit creates possibilities for sustained life and work achievement and a model for self-leadership and the leadership of others.

Daily Healthy Habits

Quality and consistency of our health habits are the keys. A daily regimen of customized physical, emotional, and spiritual nourishment is a direct cause of high energy, enthusiasm, stamina and sustained achievement.

Each of us has to develop our own *customized* combination of enriching body-mind-spirit experiences and activities. To the degree that we practice consistent habits of exercise, nutrition, and mind development, we strengthen our independent minds, our exemplary relationships, and our gifts and talents.

About Stress

The highest achievers in our research (those who have mindsets and behaviors consistently in development, craft, and artistry) share an overall strategy that they claim provides their sustained health and fitness: they differentiate between positive stress (termed eustress) and negative stress (termed distress) and handle each differently.

Eustress is healthy, challenging us to do more, improve, and achieve. Eustress is handled well when we're confident, proactive, and creating opportunities for growth and learning.

Distress is unhealthy, creating tension, conflict, and anxiety. Distress appears when we are underprepared, distracted, late, unskilled, negative, lack confidence, or are dealing with a difficult issue.

The high achievers focus consistently on increasing eustress, experiences that are creative, stimulating, exciting, and rewarding. In turn, they decrease or eliminate distress, those experiences that are undesirable, unrewarding, and drain their energy. They control both types of stress.

Reflections on Health and Fitness

Your body-mind-spirit health requires the highest priority. It rewards you with the continual option to participate in the fullest range of life activities. Your goal at all times, under all conditions, is optimal physical, mental, and emotional fitness. It's a daily challenge with immeasurable payoffs and learning when you take action. It is the foundation that gives added strength to the other catalysts of inspiration. Good health is a major influence on optimism. It's the anchor variable for a life of sustained effort and accomplishment, for getting the most out of every moment you are living.

Just In Case

We might be living over,
or ...
this could be all we get.
I mustn't live as though the first were true.

Mustn't drive by the fence where my mare stands
two hundred yards away,
and in my certainty that she won't respond,
miss her trotting over to me,
miss the nuzzle,
and the magical arrival of the gelding,
out of nowhere, to join in the reunion...
miss, as I jump the fence to leave,
the two turn to face the herd,
as if summoned by silent invitation,
breaking into spontaneous flight, side by side,
hooves kicking up meadow with their speed,
evening sun glinting off their backs.

I mustn't be lured by some finish line, a promise of escape,
by pasturing myself,
relinquishing and even devaluing the life I've made,
and in that abandonment find myself sequestered
from everything else,
from artistry,
from the spontaneity of my horses ...
a sort of pride in achieving nothing...no thing.

I mustn't miss the extraordinary,
the deep existence,
exhilaration offset by heartbreak,
play a counterbalance to work,
each fully tasted to weariness...
I mustn't miss this,
and end up simply walking my dogs through the streets...
wearing that leisurely badge of artlessness.

We may be living over
and over,
each successive life
a change to evolve,
if only modestly,

but just in case,
I mustn't miss this one. [22]

---

[22] Michael Adams, 2010.

V

Action and Leverage

The Artistry Ecosystem

Your catalysts of inspiration---1) your strong, independent mind, 2) your team of exemplary relationships, 3) your well-developed gifts and talents, and 4) your excellent health and fitness---form an powerful ecosystem that broadens and strengthens your thinking, belief system, and behavior.

When practiced, each catalyst strengthens each other catalyst. An independent mind attracts other unconventional thinkers and builds exemplary relationships. In turn, these outstanding people stretch everyone's creative thinking, gifts, and talents, further strengthening their independent thinking. And health and fitness provides the strong foundation for sustained effort.

Over time, the action catalysts become interwoven *habits* that build momentum, tap greater potential, and encourage you to pursue your artistry.

Independent Thinking

+

Inspirational People

+

Developed Gifts

+

Health

creates

A R T I S T R Y

Life Is Tough. This is Good.

Adversity brings opportunities for learning and growth. Facing challenges, solving problems, and handling difficult times are daily life experiences that demand action. Growing through struggles avoids the numbing effect that has many people acting like pawns on the chessboard of life, moving only at the discretion of outside forces and espousing *impossible* as a frequent response to life situations. Struggles help you build a habit of giving your best and building your confidence. You get tough.

People who offset the unconscious conspiracy of good enough and succeed against challenging limitations and difficult odds embody courage, commitment, unwavering optimism, and chutzpah. They represent all ages, all professions, all levels of education, and some with disabilities, life-threatening diseases, impoverished lifestyles, or disadvantaged environments.

These individuals are undeterred by challenging circumstances. They accept the cards they have been dealt them, realize that limitations are not real unless they believe them, and choose ways to learn and grow through the difficult times. Rather than being blocked by obstacles, they see opportunities and what they need to do to be successful, whether that requires more skills, more knowledge, or more effort.

These individuals defy limitation and show a persistent dedication to learning, growth, and excellence. They live in the mindsets, intentions, and actions of development, craft and artistry. The challenges of life make them stronger.

Action Leverage for Added Results

Leverage is a powerful factor in taking action and achieving results. It is the process of using a small amount of time and effort to have a large impact.

It's the awareness and skill set that, when well developed, results in significant increases in performance and achievement. It's the constant ability to think for yourself, evaluate potential benefit versus costs, and choose the most efficient path to achievement.

The most effective principles of leverage used by participants in my research projects who maintained mindsets of development, craft, and artistry included five daily practices:

1. Say No

2. Keep Life Simple.

3. Fly Under The Radar

4. Keep Faith Amidst Criticism and Doubt

5. Constantly Rebound and Stay in Line

1. Say No. Perhaps the most important factor in leveraging time and energy is the skill and courage to say No. This action protects your higher priorities, allows time for new and spontaneous opportunities, and optimizes time for learning and growth. Beware of accepting innumerable requests for your time and energy to meet the needs of others. These requests come from all parts of life---work, social, community, volunteer efforts, and family.

Not being able to say no is characteristic of a good enough mentality, of not being clear as to what is your best use of time and effort. Protect what's most important in life, what needs to be your focus of time and energy. Say no to any request that does not contribute directly to your higher priorities.

2. Keep Life Simple. Consistently focus on simplicity in all matters, on how to make the seemingly complex easier and more understandable. Avoid the dramatic, the tendency to exaggerate the problem, to emphasize the obstacles. Use simplicity to determine the easiest path to accomplish what you are facing. Identify your key tasks, prioritize them, and do each in order of importance. You'll be impressed at the quality and quantity of your added achievements.

3. Fly Under The Radar. There is a Japanese proverb that reminds us that the nail that stands highest gets hit first. Let the limelight shine on others. Fly low, out of sight.

Forget the social applause that comes with hyping your intentions, actions, or achievements. Reject the false rewards of outside accolades. Your strongest recognition comes from within.

4. Keep Faith Amidst Criticism and Doubt. When we pursue a life of learning, growth, and excellence, we often find ourselves subject to questioning and critical comments from others. In most cases, such criticism comes from those who dwell in good enough or negative mindsets. They are the obstacles that Albert Einstein labels as mediocrities in, "Great spirits have always found violent opposition from mediocrities. The latter cannot understand it when a man does not thoughtlessly submit to hereditary prejudices but honestly and courageously uses his intelligence."

Consistent achievers are so committed to their compelling purpose that they are immune to misplaced criticism. While they acknowledge and consider such feedback, it is not an obstacle that deters them. They are centered in their purpose, are clear in their thinking, and stand tall amidst the deluge of outside opinion.

It is not the critic who counts; not the man who points out how the strong man stumbles, or where the doer of deeds could have done them better.

The credit belongs to the man who is actually in the arena, whose face is marred by dust and sweat and blood; who strives valiantly; who errs, who comes short again and again, because there is no effort without error and shortcoming; but who does actually strive to do the deeds; who knows great enthusiasms, the great devotions; who spends himself in a worthy cause; who at the best knows in the end the triumph of high achievement, and who at the worst, if he fails, at least fails while daring greatly, so that his place shall never be with those cold and timid souls who neither know victory nor defeat. [23]

---

[23] Teddy Roosevelt, speech excerpt, *Citizenship In A Republic*, Paris, 1910.

A significant challenge is to achieve artistry amidst doubt and criticism. Here is a story that grew out of our research project on mindsets and how they produce different levels of performance in athletic teams.

Let there be a college football team with a consistent losing record, multiple year disappointments, a loss of student support and Coach C's time has come once again. The odds are against him. The doubt among alumni, administration, and students is clear. The slightest change he might make is subject to criticism. And yet, he turns minds around, brings a refreshed sense of possibility, and creates a culture of development, craft, and artistry. The team's young players and coaches experience a renewed sense of optimism and success. He has done it time after time---first in the NAIA Division, then Division III, then Division I FCS, then Division I.

The story has been similar at each institution: a number of losing seasons, the current coach retires or moves on, a search process identifies Coach C and his rare combination of technical skills, self-confidence, and leadership. He readily embraces this primary calling to develop men of character and leadership.

And then the process begins. First, there's a call to set personal, academic, and football goals higher than anyone expects. Higher. Higher. There's much talk among most of the returning players that the higher goals are beyond their reach. Second, there's Coach C's Leadership Development System that integrates select principles of leadership, achievement, and character at each stage of physical, psychological, and spiritual training. As usual, there is skepticism this new coach is asking too much. Some previous assistant coaches leave on their own, while others are released by the Athletic Director. Coach C brings in coaching replacements who believe in his system and can't wait to implement it. The word spreads among walk-ons that there's a new guy in town and he believes in possibilities. The buzz has begun.

Slowly, one by one, players and coaches begin to understand that their achievement in any endeavor is greatly influenced by what they believe is possible. Coach C's efforts to show what's possible in individual and team achievement extend to an annual, challenging trip to Colorado and the summiting of Pikes Peak by seniors and the coaching staff. The players begin to see improvements in their academics, on the field, in their personal lives---a little here, a little there---a greater commitment of time and effort in studying, more energy at football practice, a bit more organization at home.

Coach C is unwavering in his optimism, relentless in his expectation of excellence by everyone, and constantly focusing on possibility, and the coaching assistants, players, the student body, faculty, and administrators are showing their support. There's a bit of swagger around the campus.

Once again, Coach C has a new mission in Division I, another challenging assignment---how to deal with a recent history of losing seasons, of dispirited players, and a disengaged student body.

His rare ability to build a winning culture, to alter the thinking and lift the spirits of all concerned, and to create achievement that covers the field of competition, the classroom, the student body, the faculty, and administrators is coming to bear once again. Stay tuned for excellence. [24]

---

[24] Kunkel, *The Performance Distribution Study:* Chris Creighton, 1998-present.

5. Constantly Rebound and Stay In Line. Brian Tracy offers sage advice on how to get to the front of what he calls *the buffet line of life*. He suggests you must first get in line, and second, you must stay in line.

Most people fail to even get in line. For those who do, impatience or giving up prevails. At the first obstacle, many leave the line. However, you must commit to the *sustained* pursuit of solving whatever you are facing, of rebounding from hard knocks and setbacks, of accomplishing whatever your intent.

You must stay in the line of life's consistent challenges because,

> Nothing in this world can take the place of persistence.
> Talent will not, nothing is more common
> than unsuccessful men with talent.
> Genius will not, unrewarded genius is almost a proverb.
> Education will not. The world is full of educated derelicts.
> Persistence and determination alone are omnipotent.
> The slogan "Press On" has solved and always
> will solve the problems of the human race.
> Calvin Coolidge

A colleague of mine, Clayton, told me a fascinating personal experience he had with the power of saying no to distractions, keeping the faith, and staying in line. Throughout high school Clayton dreamed of being a cadet at the United States Military Academy at West Point. Since appointments to the academy are made through members of Congress and the Senate, Clayton applied to his Congressman in Maryland and received a 3rd alternate appointment the fall of his senior year of high school. This put him fourth in line for the nomination behind a principal appointee and the 1st and 2nd alternates.

Unfortunately, the principal appointee accepted the nomination and all alternate appointments were closed. Clayton decided to attend Johns Hopkins University and seek a nomination to West Point the following year. He applied the next fall and was given a 2nd alternate appointment. With the principal and 1st alternate appointees ahead of him, his chances again were slim. His hopes were lifted when he was notified that the principal nominee had decided to attend the Naval Academy and that now he was the 1st alternate.

As a 1st alternate, Clayton was eligible to take the academic exam in case the principal declined the appointment at the last minute. He did well on the academic exam; however, the new principal appointee accepted the nomination and Clayton was facing another year of waiting and applying again.

It was now the end of May, only 5 weeks before the new cadets reported to West Point. Clayton told me he clearly remembers feeling so close to achieving his goal and yet so far from realizing his dream. While he was required to apply to the Congressman or Senator who represented his district in Maryland, he had a sense there must be another way to pursue admission to the academy.

So Clayton drove to Washington D.C. on five consecutive days in mid-May, spending his time walking the halls of Congress and the Senate, knocking on office doors, and telling his story. He became skilled in approaching each office, often waiting until the executive assistant left on an errand before entering. This gave him the opportunity to meet the Congressman or Senator in each office. Over the five days, Clayton kept close count of his visits to 143 Congressional and Senate offices, meeting over 100 aides and assistants, and 64 politicians with no success.

On the afternoon of the fifth day, he entered a Congressional office, briefly explained his situation to the executive assistant. She told him to have a seat and she would speak to the Congressman. In a few minutes, she returned and escorted him into the Congressman's office.

The Congressman asked Clayton to tell his story. After describing his challenge and answering several questions, there was a lengthy silence. The Congressman shared a story about his childhood dreams and how his pastor had been a particular mentor, encouraging him to reach high in life and that message had changed his life.

The Congressman then walked around the side of his desk, looked Clayton directly in the eyes and said, "Son, I have a vacancy in my appointments. I'm impressed with you, your attitude and commitment, and I am honored to appoint you this year to West Point."

Clayton said he was stunned, somewhat unsure of exactly what the Congressman meant. Then the Congressman reached out, shook his hand, and said, "I'm counting on you to represent me well. My assistant will handle all the details. I wish you the best."

An added twist to this story is that this incident occurred when racial discrimination was rampant throughout our country. However, it was Congressman Adam Clayton Powell (D, NY), a distinguished African-American representing Harlem, who appointed Clayton, a white young man previously unknown to him, to the United States Military Academy while saying "I am honored to appoint you". Clayton admits that, even to this day, he is moved that Congressman Powell was honored to appoint him.

Clayton achieved a dream because he rebounded from 143 rejections, stayed in line, and eventually crossed paths with an exemplary individual, a mentor of the moment. Clayton subsequently graduated from West Point, served in the armed forces, completed graduate study, dedicated his career to the field of higher education, and continues to improve the lives of others.

Clayton stayed in line and subsequently joined "The Long Gray Line".

Reflections on Artistry in Action

The five actions of leverage enhance the impact of the catalysts of inspiration. The four catalysts are the strategies that inspire and are the framework for excellence. The five actions make their implementation more inefficient and effective. Working together, they train your body-mind-spirit into *best performance* across all facets of your life.

During my career spanning nearly four decades now, I have witnessed a number of outstanding individuals who used the catalysts of inspiration and the actions of leverage consistently with significant success. I also observed a number of small teams whose members displayed mindsets in development, craft, and artistry. They worked together and achieved dramatically more than other groups in the good enough and negativity categories. What is most rare, however, is to find a group of individuals that has some early achievement and, over an extended period of time, grows into a large, highly successful organization and maintains a culture of artistry, integrity, and financial success.

The following is the story of one of those rare gems of a company that was defined by the four catalysts of inspiration.

Newman and Associates, an investment banking company in Denver, Colorado, was formed in 1979 by a handful of young entrepreneurs who saw possibilities of creating new products and meaningful customer service in a traditional industry. They faced formidable odds and were strongly discouraged by old timers in the industry.

However, these were different thinkers, mavericks of sort, rebels, hungry and foolish. What was most impressive about these team members was their respect and support for each other. While certainly focused on the potential financial rewards for their efforts, their relationships with each other came first. Through the challenging early years of building their company, they stuck to a code of ethics that honored their relationships with one another, with their employees, and with their clients. The word spread quickly that this young team was different, innovative, dedicated to outstanding client service, and of the highest integrity.

The practice of the catalysts of inspiration was imbedded in the company's DNA. The senior team constantly encouraged each other and all levels of employees toward *independent thinking* and the questioning of conventional wisdom. The combination of different personalities and unique thinking was an anomaly in this staid business industry. These were unconventional minds, constantly looking for new ideas and creative insights for products and services. Part of their success was due to their ability to channel their creative, independent energies productively. In addition, the senior staff modeled integrity and high moral character in all their endeavors. This provided the basis for a strong *circle of exemplary relationships* that consistently drew to it those new employees who were committed to discovering their best. Even at times when there were disappointments in individual performance, the process for handling those was professional, respectful, and just.

The catalyst of *pursuing artistry through emphasizing gifts and talents* was a basic expectation for each employee. The focus of being your best under all conditions was consistently discussed and reinforced in all company communication, training, and events.

Finally, Newman and Associates was dedicated to a culture of *health and fitness*. They sponsored health memberships, registration fees for sports events, even some on-site medical services for all staff. The annual flu shot clinic in the corporate boardroom was deeply appreciated by the staff. Also, executives encouraged employees to use flex-time to accommodate personal and family needs and covered all staff during injury or sickness circumstances.

From 1979 to 1998, the company grew steadily to over 360 employees, all the while building a culture of high performance and personal excellence. Newman's success, both in the development of its outstanding workforce and in its financial performance, was unequaled in the industry. In collaborative processes with all production team members, managers set seemingly unreachable goals and achieved them time and time again. Ultimately, this unparalleled track record attracted a large international conglomerate that purchased the company in 1998. As evidence of the high quality of leadership, the entire senior staff was contracted to remain in place and continue to serve.

Newman and Associates was organized and developed by the founders with the belief that there is a artist in everyone and, given a culture of human and business excellence, the artistry in each employee would be expressed. I observed this phenomenon time and time again at all staff levels. The company receptionist, a graphic designer, a number of investment bankers, and administrative personnel explained to me that they saw themselves as the CEOs of their responsibilities. They pointed out that they were primarily in control of their performance and productivity and thoroughly enjoyed their opportunities to contribute to a company that was dedicated to such high standards of excellence.

The exemplary men and women leaders of Newman and Associates honored their independent thinking, created a culture of artistry, and brought out the best in themselves, associates, and clients, making a significant contribution to their industry. They did what others said could not be done.

Unconventional wisdom. Excellence. Best. Artistry. Inspiration. [25]

[25] Kunkel, *The Performance Distribution Study:* Newman and Associates, 1992-2004.

VI

One More Thing

You have a masterpiece inside you, too, you know.
One unlike any that has ever been created,
or ever will be.
And remember:
If you go to your grave
without painting your masterpiece,
it will not get painted.
No one else can paint it.
Only you. [26]

You are one of a kind. Rare. Exceptional. Singular. In all the history of the world there has never been anyone like you. And in all history to come, there never will be another you.

As such, you have an opportunity that is yours and yours alone. It's your chance to tap hidden dimensions of potential, creativity, and excellence within yourself and bring them all to life, to understand that your artistry is defined as excelling within yourself, not in competition with others. It's the opportunity to experience your true best throughout your life.

---

[26] MacKenzie, *Orbiting the Giant Hairball*, (passage on his funeral leaflet, July 26, 1999), 224.

Your time is limited,
so don't waste it living someone else's life.
Don't be trapped by dogma, which is living
with the results of other peoples' thinking.
Don't let the noise of others' opinions
drown out your own inner voice.
And, most important, have the courage
to follow your heart and intuition.
They somehow already know
what you truly want to become.
Everything else is secondary. [27]

[27] Jobs, Commencement Address, 2005.

Your Possibility

Create a life that honors, supports, and strengthens your uniqueness, rejects the forces of conformity, and highlights what's possible for you, others, and the world around you.

Amidst the mind-numbing chatter of external voices, think for yourself and discover your own way.

Pursue your compelling purpose, a work and life path that encourages your unique self to flourish so you are truly you and the only one who does what you do and how you do it.

The world needs you at your best. There are family members, friends, colleagues, and even acquaintances who are counting on you to model the kind of thinking and actions that helps them see their possibilities, purpose, and meaning and achieve excellence.

Finally, with my unwavering belief in the power of your independent mind, your unique gifts and talents, your potential exemplary team, and your commitment to holistic health and fitness, I leave you with three thoughts:

Who will you inspire?

How will you lift the human spirit of those around you?

What will you do to improve the human condition?

Selected Bibliography

Clark, Glenn. *The Man Who Tapped the Secrets of the Universe*. Waynesboro, VA: University of Science and Philosophy, 1946.

Frankl, Viktor. *Man's Search for Meaning*. New York: Simon & Schuster, 1959.

Gardner, Howard. *Frames of Mind*. New York: Basic Books, 1983.

Gardner, John. *Self-Renewal*. New York: Harper & Row Publishers, 1965.

Hennessy, Leslie A. (2014). *Decision Making and Creativity: A Qualitative Study of MacArthur Fellows* (3580979). Available from Dissertations & Theses @ University of San Diego; ProQuest Dissertations & Theses Full Text; ProQuest Dissertations & Theses Global. (1544448566).

Kahneman, Daniel. *Thinking Fast and Slow*. New York: Farrar, Straus, and Giroux, 2011.

MacKenzie, Gordon. *Orbiting the Giant Hairball*. New York: Viking Penguin, 1998.

O'Neil, John. *The Paradox of Success*, New York: G. P. Putnam Sons, 1993.

Perkins, Dennis N. T. *Leading at the Edge*. New York: AMACOM, 2000.

Phillips, Michael and Rasberry, Salli. *Honest Business*. New York: Random House, Inc. 1981.

Ray, Michael. *The Highest Goal*. San Francisco: Berrett-Koehler Publishers, 2004.

Pink, Daniel H. *A Whole New Mind*. New York: Penguin Group, 2005.

Sygall, Susan and Spillman, Ken. *No Ordinary Days*. Eugene, OR: New Hebrides Press, 2014.

Zander, Rosamund Stone and Zander, Benjamin. *The Art of Possibility*. New York: Penguin Group, 2000.

Acknowledgments (who inspires the author)

No man is an island; no man stands alone.

Leslie Hennessy - life partner, best friend, teammate, integrity, challenges conventional thinking (especially moi), models learning and excellence, perceptive coach, inspiration, Dr L.

Scotty, Kerry, Tom, Kara, Clay, Avery, Grace, Hudson - exemplary family members, energy, excitement, laughter, accelerated learners - Terrific!

Alison Hennessy – impressive, confident, never met a country she didn't like, adventurer, reliable, entrepreneurial mind, thinks why not?

Sherwood - once in a lifetime canine companion, humble, reliable, regal, noble, epitome of excellence, artistry in service to Penrose Hospital rehabilitation patients, Colorado State Service Hero 2011.

BJ & Michael Adams – the Team, life visionaries, embrace higher purpose in business, see possibility, musical souls, introspective, constant learning.

Scot Barker - friend, classmate, subtle leader, honors humanity in workforce, committed to human development while pursuing corporate success.

Robert Beale - friend, colleague, outstanding business strategist, integrates spiritual dimension into career and life success.

Jack Gibb - mentor, sage, friend, visionary, so ahead of his time, brilliant insights re trust levels create behavioral outcomes and cultural impact.

John Jones - mentor, friend, colleague, renaissance man, acute intuition about human behavior, vision of one world, abundance mentality.

Andy & Jean Kremm – integrity, 60+ year partners, youthful lifestyles, voracious readers, avid learners, compassionate, gracious, Beat Navy!

Ann Kunkel – shining family star, lifelong learner, sees bright side, happy soul, model of encouragement, gives positive reinforcement continually.

Patrick Owens - brotherhood, exemplary teacher, connects with kids, simplicity, always count on him, that's EL not LE, laughter center.

Steve Sinton – friend, problem solver, unbounded creativity, multiple skill sets, ambassador for land trusts, helps under any circumstances, integrity.

Joe Turcotte - special friend, ultimate achiever, Ironman, reliability, versatile competencies, well-read, positive force, has life achievement PhD.

Ron Wisner – special friend, caring, thoughtful, ultimate Dean, students first, multisport athlete, grand master, credibility, positive force, loved life.

About The Author

Husband, Dad, Grandy, with some wild and crazy friends. Loves all puppies, goldens, labs, and is the unofficial distractor of his wife's dedicated training of service dogs for Canine Companions for Independence (CCI).

Wonders what's possible in all situations. Biased advocate for creative, eccentric thinkers and artists in all professions.

Life focus is using the power of the mind to offset societal conditioning and pursue one's best, one's excellence, one's artistry.

Founded Catalyst International in 1978, providing research and training in human behavior, performance, and achievement. Has served CEOs, managers, and staff in US and European corporations, entrepreneurial ventures, healthcare and educational institutions, NCAA athletic teams, and select non-profits. Current focus includes individuals challenged by disabilities and wounded warriors.

Graduated from the United States Military Academy, West Point; served in military intelligence in the US Air Force. MS - Education (Univ of Southern California). National Defense Fellow: MBA and PhD (Univ of Denver) - emphasis on innovation, leadership, and human performance. Management consultant - Deloitte. Staff - University of California, Berkeley.

Lives with his wife in Colorado Springs. Enjoys running, cycling, hiking, rowing, and cross-country skiing. Hopes for a spontaneous gig playing the piano or keyboard for the Eagles in the Hollywood Bowl, fulfilling his dream of ultimate achievement.

Catalyst International
Colorado Springs CO

catalyst.rk@icloud.com

www.catalyst-international.net